The Love of Three Oranges

(one-act version)

A SHORT COMEDY BY

Hillary DePiano

BASED ON A SCENARIO BY CARLO GOZZI

The Rules in Brief

- DO NOT perform this Play without obtaining prior permission from Playscripts, and without paying the required royalty.

- DO NOT photocopy, scan, or otherwise duplicate any part of this book.

- DO NOT alter the text of the Play, change a character's gender, delete any dialogue, cut any music, or alter any objectionable language, unless explicitly authorized by Playscripts.

- DO provide the required credit to the author(s) and the required attribution to Playscripts in all programs and promotional literature associated with any performance of this Play.

Copyright Basics

This Play is protected by United States and international copyright law. These laws ensure that authors are rewarded for creating new and vital dramatic work, and protect them against theft and abuse of their work.

A play is a piece of property, fully owned by the author, just like a house or car. You must obtain permission to use this property, and must pay a royalty fee for the privilege—whether or not you charge an admission fee. Playscripts collects these required payments on behalf of the author.

Anyone who violates an author's copyright is liable as a copyright infringer under United States and international law. Playscripts and the author are entitled to institute legal action for any such infringement, which can subject the infringer to actual damages, statutory damages, and attorneys' fees. A court may impose statutory damages of up to $150,000 for willful copyright infringements. U.S. copyright law also provides for possible criminal sanctions. Visit the website of the U.S. Copyright Office (www.copyright.gov) for more information.

THE BOTTOM LINE: If you break copyright law, you are robbing a playwright and opening yourself to expensive legal action. Follow the rules, and when in doubt, ask us.

To Steve, who loves this play at any length.

Cast of Characters

NARRATOR

SILVIO, King of Hearts, dressed like the playing card

PANTALONE, adviser to the King

LEANDRO, First Minister

PRINCESS CLARICE, niece to the King

BRIGHELLA, Leandro and Clarice's dimwitted minion

PRINCE TARTAGLIA, Jack of Hearts, dressed like the playing card when formal

TRUFFALDINO, a famous jester, secretly employed by Celio

SMERALDINA, Fata Morgana's slightly less dimwitted minion

FATA MORGANA, an evil witch

A GATE, of unspeakable horror

A DONKEY, of unutterable horror

A ROPE, of horror that cannot possibly be spoken

A COOK, of about average horror

CREONTA, another evil witch

PRINCESS NINETTA, formerly an orange

PRINCESS NICOLETTA, also formerly an orange

PRINCESS LINETTA, yet another former orange

MUSICIAN

ASSORTED COUNTRY BUMPKINS, PALACE GUARDS, SERVANTS, and FEAST GUESTS

Place

A fairy tale kingdom.

Time

The time is the imaginary present.

Production Notes

The following are suggestions, tips, hints and warnings about performing this production:

Setting

For the original production of this play, Guerry Hood designed a raised platform with ramps leading up to it which was the basis for all scenes. It was painted such that it could look like indoors or outdoors depending on the lighting of the scene. The backdrop of all scenes was a large book, made to look like a dusty antique volume with the title written on the front in gold. The play began with the book closed and then the narrator would turn the "pages" before each scene. Each page was a painted flat of the background of the scene. For simplicity's sake, our production used only a general internal palace room for all scenes in the palace, a general outside scene of the forest, the inside of Morgana's castle, and Creonta's yard. After Creonta's, the narrator began to turn the book backwards (i.e., two pages at once to get back to the forest and then back to the palace for the final scene). This way, when it came time for him to close the book at the end of the curtain call, it was only one page thick and thus much faster and easier to turn.

For all forest scenes, we had a large signpost (for hiding behind) that you could turn in many directions depending on which way the characters were coming from and a log large enough for all three oranges to sit on at once. These were moved around the forest alternately depending on the scene to denote different parts of the woods.

Musician / Music

An unseen presence who furnishes his commentary on the scenes with music from vaudeville to the soap opera, he has a tendency to pad his part. Can be anything from a single person with a keyboard to a small band or even canned musical effects. It is, however, preferable if the musician is real person. Not only does this allow for the musician to perform live, adjusting to the performance as it happens, but it also gives the music a personality of its own and makes its appearances in the story less sound cue and more like an impish commentary on the action itself. The original run utilized a single keyboardist who was mostly hidden from the audience by a black mesh curtain. The musician is in direct contact with the Narrator at all times, while the other characters only acknowledge him when he is particularly obtrusive.

Improvisation

Improvisation, while such an integral element of Gozzi's original text, here provides some pitfalls. The scenes most designed to be extemporaneous such as the chases and fights are the most dangerous to be done so. While improvisation is encouraged in the rehearsal process, ensure that the action of your chases and fights is set by dress rehearsals to minimize injury to the performers.

Puppets

There is a good deal of puppetry potential throughout this production, most obviously with Ninetta's transformation into the dove. Preferably, the actress playing Ninetta performs the dove puppet herself which allows the audience to see the emotions of the dove as they play out on the actress's face. Her transformation is simply tossing the dove aside when she becomes a princess again.

Besides the obvious opportunities with the donkey, gate and rope, the original production also included hobby horses that served as Tartaglia and Truffaldino's steeds on their quest. The actors mounted and rode them as if they were real horses and manipulated them like they were puppets both while riding and after dismounting. This also provided some extra comedy for, once the convention is established, while Targalia keeps with it, Truffaldino abandons it.

Magic and Special Effects

An effect doesn't need to be costly to be special and you can accomplish amazing things even with no budget or tech. It's the actors that are the real wizards and they'll be the ones that convince the audience that they're seeing magic. Never underestimate the power of a well rehearsed action and reaction. By itself, an actor that makes a slap motion towards another across the stage isn't anything special but if the target of the gesture reacts as if they've really been mystically hit, they'll sell the illusion to the audience. The real secret lies in nailing the timing, committing to the action and doing broad and obvious gestures so there's no mistaking what's going on.

Beyond long distance stage combat, simple sound and lighting cues can enhance the performance as long as they are timed just right. Simple tricks such as tossing a handful of sparkles or firing a handheld confetti cannon are technically simple to implement, inexpensive to acquire and can look very impressive from out in the audience when coupled with good performances. Don't be afraid to experiment. Even if your effects fall short and end up more "special" than intended, failed magic still looks better than none at all and the chaos will be in the spirit of the show anyway.

THE LOVE OF THREE ORANGES
(ONE-ACT VERSION)

by Hillary DePiano

BASED ON A SCENARIO BY CARLO GOZZI

Prologue

(The curtain is already open as the audience enters. The backdrop is a large book with "The Love of Three Oranges" written on the cover. It is closed. The house lights remain on while the NARRATOR runs onto the stage in distress. He wears an ordinary suit and tie as if he isn't part of the play at all. He scans the crowd. What to do? He begins, quietly at first, to try to get the audience's attention.)

NARRATOR. Ladies and gentlemen! Excuse me! Can I have your attention please? Thank you. I'm sorry, but it seems we have a situation on our hands. You see, right now, all the characters that make up this story are hiding on the other side of these curtains. And quite honestly it's because they are scared of you. They suspect you've figured out by now that this is a Commedia dell'Arte play and are edging towards the door. They think you don't want to hear a story as old and musty as theirs. After all, our story has been told since before any of you were even born and in a world that demands the new and immediate, I suppose our simple old tale can't compete. But in the face of so much horror and the world weighing down on us, I refuse to believe there is no place for laughter! Levity is what saves us from the load and there is and will always be room in this world for amusement simply for amusement's sake! I'm sure the characters that make up this tale will be ready to begin as soon as they hear you call for them. Your applause and laughter is the life that courses through their veins. So, are you willing to give our old story a new chance? *(He encourages them to clap.* CHARACTERS *begin to peek tentatively around the sides of the stage at the sound. To the light booth:)* So, can we please have the lights down some? *(Lights dim.)* Excellent. You will witness many strange things this evening and we ask you to please check your disbelief at the door of the theatre. I'd like to tell you what this story is about, but I'm a little afraid you'll laugh at me. Because the story is…well it's mostly about oranges… and happiness…and a little about love. Maybe you should just see for yourself. So sit back like you were a little child on your grandfather's knee and let me tell you a story like you've never heard before.

(As he says his final line, he opens the book to the backdrop of the castle. He claps once to signal the beginning of the play. Chaos as CHARACTERS *emerge from all sides, pushing scenery and carrying props, costumes and other actors, bumping into each other in their excitement to begin the show. The* THREE WOMEN *who later play the oranges, in their Act 1 costumes, not as the oranges, skip across the stage hand-in-hand. Some of the actors preset the still-as-statues frozen* KING *and* PANTALONE *and position them for the scene. During the madness, the* NARRATOR *stops* TRUFFALDINO, *points* TARTAGLIA *out to him and then the two part,* TRUFFALDINO *offstage, the* NARRATOR *to the audience where he takes a seat to watch. No other character acknowledges the* NARRATOR *as anything more than an obstacle in their path. They set up for the first scene and clear the stage and the* NARRATOR *claps which brings the* KING *and* PANTALONE *to life.)*

Scene 1

(A room in the palace. KING SILVIO *and* PANTALONE.*)*

SILVIO, KING OF HEARTS. Oh, Pantalone! My only child, Prince Tartaglia, the heir to my throne, is still sick after all these months. He lies in his room day in and day out, too ill to leave, and yet we still do not know what has made him so sick.

PANTALONE. Your majesty. I don't mean to be indiscreet, but could the illness be something that you contracted in your youth?

KING. Of course not! I have always been faithful, completely faithful, to my wife, the Queen of Hearts. May she rest in peace.

PANTALONE. Hmm. Well, let's not underestimate the prince. Maybe he got a dose himself.

KING. Prince Tartaglia has never known love. *(Sappy music.)* He is still waiting for someone or something to animate his heart. *(Music stops abruptly.)* No, Pantalone. I have had him examined by all the greatest doctors in the land and for once they all agree.

PANTALONE. And what do they agree it is?

KING. It is an extremely grave, and most probably fatal, case of *(Big dramatic pause:)* terminal hypochondria. *(Dramatic flourish of music.)*

PANTALONE. Hypochondria?

KING. Yes! The doctors say there is nothing they can do to cure him. Oh, my poor son! If we could just make him laugh, I know it would make him feel better. Just a little smile on his face would be a sign of an improvement. But it is impossible, he is so very miserable. Ah, it grieves me, Pantalone. I'm such an old man and my only son lies on his deathbed, which means that the crown will pass to my niece, Princess Clarice, who just generally creeps me out. Death by hypochondria!

PANTALONE. Sire, you must stop grieving like this or you'll be on your deathbed too. How do you expect to get the prince to laugh when the whole court is in mourning? There is hope! The great clown Truffaldino has arrived at the court today. What I suggest is…have a party! We'll have games and a tournament! It could be a masked ball! With all the merriment of the costumes and feast, the prince is bound to at least chuckle. If anyone can cure the prince it'll be Truffaldino.

KING. Hmmm. There is something in what you say…

PANTALONE. What have you got to lose? We've tried everything else!

KING. But the boy is sick! All the noise and festivities might make him worse.

PANTALONE. But sick with hypochondria!

KING. Terminal hypochondria. Yes.

PANTALONE. That means it's all in his mind!

KING. Hmmm…well, we'll try it. I will speak with this Truffaldino immediately.

> *(They start to exit just as* LEANDRO *enters.)*

KING. Ah, Leandro. I was just about to give orders for some festivities. We are having a court banquet and a masked ball with entertainment for the prince starring the famous clown Truffaldino and we are having it tonight. And another thing. I also hereby decree that whoever can make the prince laugh, by whatever means, will get a huge prize.

PANTALONE. An excellent idea, your majesty.

KING. Of course it is, that's why I'm king.

PANTALONE. Oh, your highness, you are such a card.

KING. Shut up, Pantalone.

> *(The* KING *and* PANTALONE *exit.)*

LEANDRO. *(Calls after them:)* Your highness, I beg you to reconsider! Poor Prince Tartaglia is a very sick boy. *(They are gone.)* Why won't that little brat drop dead already? Damn that meddling Pantalone!

And where did this insipid clown Truffaldino come from? What rotten luck to have the clown show up now. Is someone interfering with our plans?

(PRINCESS CLARICE enters and runs to LEANDRO.)

CLARICE. Oh, my most precious! Love you! Kisses! Cheek! Cheek! Lips! Fish face!

LEANDRO. Shnookums, perhaps we should not be so free with affections until the prince is dead.

CLARICE. O foo. OK. But I am tired of waiting. I want to get married now.

LEANDRO. Patience, my little peachy blossom. I have enlisted a very powerful ally, one who will help tip the balance of power in our favor at last. That pinnacle of evil, that tower of treachery, that paragon of all things that are just generally not that nice. It is a powerful sorceress whose very name brings fear to the ears that speak it, Fata Morgana. *(Chord.)*

> *(From this point in the play on, a chord occurs after anyone says "Fata Morgana" and everyone holds a pose of fear, except for the NARRATOR who just rolls his eyes.)*

CLARICE. Ears that speak it?

LEANDRO. *(Ignores her:)* Of course the doctors think he is faking! It is through Morgana's potions that the prince has fallen ill and it will be her magic that finishes him off. And then, when the prince is dead, I will marry you and then I will be aKing!

CLARICE. And I will be Queen!

LEANDRO. *(Slightly overlapping her line:)* With me as King!

> *(They begin a full-bodied evil laugh and freeze mid-laugh when the NARRATOR suddenly claps.)*

NARRATOR. Time out! *(He walks in silence to the frozen pair and chuckles at them.)* Would you look at them? That can't be comfortable to hold for a long time. *(Tickles LEANDRO under the chin.)* Koochy koochy koo. *(Loses himself in laughter for a moment before remembering the audience.)* Oh, right! Sorry to interrupt the flow of things but I just wanted to fill you in. You see, Fata Morgana, *(Chord.)* the evil witch our frozen chums were just talking about, is obsessed with getting revenge on the Hearts for a card game gone wrong and will not rest until she has destroyed the King and his son as well. These two crown-coveting idiots are just pawns in her latest nefarious scheme.

(Sits and then claps, bringing them back to life. They fall immediately out of their laughter poses and begin looking at the sky in all directions.)

LEANDRO. What the hell was that?

CLARICE. Owie. Why do I feel so stiff?

LEANDRO. *(Touching where the* NARRATOR *tickled him:)* Something is going on here. Someone, or something is interfering. Guiding things along their own way. I don't like it. First that Truffaldino shows up out of nowhere.

CLARICE. OOOOO! I like him! He's very funny!

LEANDRO. Which, my little love bucket, is the problem! The King is right about one thing, if Tartaglia laughs, even once, Morgana's spell will be broken and I will never be King.

CLARICE. Then I will never be Queen.

LEANDRO. *(Overlap:)* Or I King. The only thing more discouraging than the appearance of this buffoon is the King's sudden whim of having a ball. And offering a prize to anyone who can make him laugh… Oh, Morgana is not going to be pleased.

(BRIGHELLA runs in.)

BRIGHELLA. Masters! Boy is Morgana ever pissed! The clown's appearance and the idea for the banquet were both planted by Celio, the good magician, and Morgana's most bitter rival. The two have never met on this earth, but he has foiled Morgana's plans for years and she vows to destroy him. He's the one who sent Truffaldino here to break the spell and to protect the prince and King.

NARRATOR. *(Claps. Everyone freezes. To audience:)* You getting all this? *(Claps again and the scene continues.)*

BRIGHELLA. But there's hope! Fata Morgana *(Chord.)* herself will be here tonight for the festivities. She sends word to attend the party as if nothing was amiss for, if he does not laugh tonight, he will be dead by morning.

(They start to cackle and the NARRATOR claps, freezing all three. As the evil trio is carried offstage while frozen, the scene changes to the hypochondriacal prince's bedchamber. PRINCE TARTAGLIA is carried onto the stage, frozen mid-sneeze. There is an I.V. with two bags on a stand attached to his arm. Next to the chair is a table piled with medicine bottles, ointments, salves, pills, spittoons, hot water bottles, and other medical paraphernalia. The NARRATOR, who has turned the page during the set-up, walks across the stage.)

Scene 2

NARRATOR. Meanwhile, on the opposite side of the castle, unaware of the plots against him, Prince Tartaglia was in misery. *(Claps.)*

(TARTAGLIA unfreezes into a big sneeze. Sad music plays. Elaborate show of blowing his nose. He is covered by a too-large blanket pulled up to his neck, with an ice pack on his head and a huge thermometer in his mouth which he takes out and checks occasionally during the scene.)

PRINCE TARTAGLIA. Poor me! *(He coughs.)* What a fate! I'm always weak, always sick, and always *(He coughs pathetically.)* ...sad. *(Sad music fades out.)*

(TRUFFALDINO enters like the announcer in a boxing match. He acts out the boxing match, playing all of the parts himself with the boxers on either side and the announcer in the center.)

TRUFFALDINO. *(As announcer:)* Ladies and gentlemen, allow me to welcome you to the bout of the century! In the left corner we have the pure bulk and destructive power of the returning champion! *(As Champ:)* UNG! I'm the champ! Watch out! I'm gonna eat your children! *(Announcer:)* And in the right corner we have an elderly British woman. *(Terrified British woman:)* Oh please gov'ner, take care! *(Announcer begins fight:)* Let's get it on! *(Bell sounds. As Champ warming up and shadowboxing:)* Show me what you got. Show me what you got! *(As British woman who mimes taking out a purse:)* Oh, I only have about four pence and twenty quid. *(Confused Champ:)* That's not really what I meant lady. *(British woman sighs dejectedly:)* Very well then.

(She suddenly pulls her arm back to punch Champ with all her might. TRUFFALDINO then jumps over and plays the Champ taking the hit in the face and getting knocked out. He then jumps back up, bows and works the crowd before confidently returning to the still stoic TARTAGLIA.)

TRUFFALDINO. Funny?

TARTAGLIA. No.

TRUFFALDINO. Very well. I don't usually use my A material on charity cases, but for you I will make an exception.

(He surveys the situation and then rips the I.V. out of TARTAGLIA's arm and, ignoring TARTAGLIA's yelp of pain, takes center stage. The rest of the stage darkens and a spotlight hits him. As he begins this next bit of dialogue, he begins to extend the I.V. stand as high as it will go and uses it as a microphone.)

TRUFFALDINO. Maestro, if you please. *(The introduction to "Send in the Clowns" begins.)* Ladies and gentlemen, what I have for you now is a story about a couple of people that just met. One of them is giving the other a bit of trouble but let's see if they can get through in the end.

> *(TRUFFALDINO then sings an abridged parody version of "Send in the Clowns" working the crowd whenever possible, working the tube as the microphone wire and waving/winking to fans and friends in the audience. He sings:)*

ISN'T IT RICH, AREN'T WE A PAIR?
ME HERE JUST CLOWNING AROUND, YOU, USING UP AIR!
SEND IN THE CLOWNS!
QUICK! SEND IN THE CLOWNS!
DON'T BOTHER. I'M HERE!

> *(The lights come up and he returns triumphantly to TARTAGLIA who is still un-amused.)*

TRUFFALDINO. Give me a break. Not even a tiny bit funny?

TARTAGLIA. No! Who the hell are you anyway?

TRUFFALDINO. Who am I? I am the internationally famous clown and wandering court jester, Truffaldino. I make everyone laugh.

TARTAGLIA. Well you don't make me laugh. *(Turns over as if he is going to sleep.)*

> *(TRUFFALDINO goes to strangle TARTAGLIA. NARRATOR clears his throat loudly. TRUFFALDINO checks himself. Sounds of music and people talking and laughing are heard offstage.)*

TRUFFALDINO. Do you hear that your highness? They are having a ball and feast in your honor! Wouldn't you like to go?

TARTAGLIA. A feast, eh? A feast in my condition? No way in hell. I'm very sick and have to stay in bed near my medicines. My precious…

> *(TARTAGLIA hugs his medicine bottles to him. TRUFFALDINO looks ready to give up and gestures to the NARRATOR that the situation is hopeless. The NARRATOR indicates that TRUFFALDINO will be in big trouble if he does not comply.)*

TRUFFALDINO. *(Losing patience:)* That's it. You're going to this stupid feast whether you like it or not!

> *(He tries to tug TARTAGLIA out of the chair but TARTAGLIA holds on too tightly and he won't budge. TRUFFALDINO then aggressively begins to throw the medicine bottles offstage.)*

TARTAGLIA. Are you crazy? What are you doing? Stop! Stop, you lunatic! My medicines! Stop! I'll die without my medicines!

(Chase music. TARTAGLIA frantically begins to try to retrieve the bottles. They chase. This chase takes them through the audience and TRUFFALDINO may even elicit the help of an audience member to hide a medicine bottle for a while. He finally tricks TARTAGLIA, catches him and swings the prince over his shoulder.)

TARTAGLIA. But I'm sick!

TRUFFALDINO. Frankly, your highness, I don't give a damn.

TARTAGLIA. Stop! Stop! I'm too sick to go out! What about my air purifier? I'll die!...

(Exit. The whole time TARTAGLIA is yelling, kicking and crying pathetically as he is carried offstage.)

Scene 3

(NARRATOR turns the page to a court room in the palace. Assorted CASTLE SERVANTS put the finishing touches on the decorations. Light music plays underneath.)

NARRATOR. And so it was time for the royal costume ball and the kingdom prepared, throwing together the most elaborate costumes they could find, all hoping to make the prince laugh to save the kingdom and claim the King's reward. Tartaglia's illness had all but outlawed happiness in the kingdom and this chance to break free from the kingdom-wide mourning and cut loose created a feeling of hope and joy in everyone. And I do mean everyone.

(He unbuttons the top of his shirt to reveal a costume underneath and then exits the stage. Guests begin to file in. CLARICE and LEANDRO are dressed in scary costumes to remind the prince of death. Everyone else in the room is wearing silly or comical masks with the exception of TRUFFALDINO, KING, and TARTAGLIA. Fanfare. Flourish. KING, TRUFFALDINO, and TARTAGLIA process in, the father and son in full playing card regalia. TARTAGLIA looks perfectly miserable and tries several times to escape but TRUFFALDINO is right behind him, jabbing his jester's stick into his back like a spear. Some guests stop TRUFFALDINO for his autograph and TARTAGLIA escapes but runs into PANTALONE who brings him right back in. The KING sits on his throne but PANTALONE and TRUFFALDINO have to tie TARTAGLIA to his and gag him to get him to stay. As they are tying up TARTAGLIA, BRIGHELLA enters wearing his usual costume and the mask from "Scream." This gets a big reaction from CLARICE and LEANDRO who are at first scared

but then approve. Among the guests is the NARRATOR *dressed similar to Where's Waldo.)*

KING. Ah beloved subjects, welcome! We are here tonight in pursuit of happiness. Most specifically, the happiness of my only son, Prince Tartaglia. Whoever can make him laugh will get this huge sack of gold. Though I say now *(Sappy music.)* that if you can touch his heart and make him happy, truly happy, my kingdom is yours. *(Music stops.)* But for now, a laugh will do. Let the entertainments begin.

> *(*TRUFFALDINO *begins to gather the guests and assign them roles in the joust.)*

TRUFFALDINO. All right let's get this show rolling. You heard the man, it's cash for laughs, people. Entertainment number one, a joust!

> *(The* NARRATOR *hands the 'SQUIRES' Truffaldino appointed their lances and they become different characters immediately. They touch the 'CHALLENGERS' and they too become their roles. The* CHALLENGERS *face off at opposite sides of the stage with their* SQUIRES. TRUFFALDINO *signals for the rest of the guests to make a drum roll and then begins to search for something in his pockets.)*

KING. The coin toss!

> *(*TRUFFALDINO *finally finds what he is looking for. It is a rubber chicken. He lifts it high above his head.)*

LEANDRO. *(Aside:)* Oh crap. This guy is good.

> *(*TRUFFALDINO *uses the chicken as the coin and tosses it high into the air and into the audience. After consulting with the audience member it landed on or near to determine the outcome [heads or tails], he shouts out the result, pointing to* CHALLENGER #1 *as the winner regardless of the outcome.* TRUFFALDINO *comes back onto the stage and begins the joust.* CHALLENGER #1 *is a very aggressive and confident fighter. She/he is always flexing, working the crowd and showing his/her teeth to the other challenger. This works best if this challenger is played by someone small and petite, perhaps one of the actresses that later play the princesses.* CHALLENGER #2, *however, is terrified of the idea of the fight and keeps trying to hide behind his/her* SQUIRE. #1's SQUIRE *tosses the lance to him/her and #1 catches it. The crowd is impressed.* #2's SQUIRE *begins to toss the lance but* CHALLENGER #2 *only cowers in fear. The crowd is disappointed.* #2's SQUIRE *finally hands* CHALLENGER #2 *the lance and he/she hands it directly back.* #2's SQUIRE *begins to walk away, realizes the switch and finally firmly hands the lance to*

CHALLENGER #2 *horizontally at chest level. CHALLENGER #2 takes it and turns around quickly, nearly hitting #2's SQUIRE who ducks quickly under it. CHALLENGER #1 advances, lance ready. CHALLENGER #2 holds the lance like a baseball bat. The crowd laughs. CHALLENGER #2 sees CHALLENGER #1 and adjusts the lance the correct way. The crowd cheers. CHALLENGER #2 is rather pleased and turns around 180 degrees quickly, assuming he/she is done, forcing everyone nearby to quickly swerve or duck to avoid the tip of his/her lance. Finally TRUFFALDINO shouts "Jousters Ready?" Once the joust begins, everyone on stage with the exception of TARTAGLIA goes into slow motion. The MUSICIAN plays "Chariots of Fire." TARTAGLIA still moves in real time, looking at the others on stage with confusion. The jousters charge and run right past each other. They turn around for another pass and on the way back, CHALLENGER #1 accidentally stabs TRUFFALDINO. Then CHALLENGER #2 stabs his other side. The jousters run out of the way and TRUFFALDINO drops the rubber chicken and then begins to fall. When he hits the ground, everyone goes back into real time and is shocked/horrified that TRUFFALDINO has been killed. He then removes the lances, uses them as ski poles and the crowd laughs with joy and relief that he is fine.)*

TRUFFALDINO. *(Aside to the KING:)* Did he laugh?

KING. *(Removing TARTAGLIA's gag:)* Wasn't that funny?

TARTAGLIA. *(Shouting:)* No. Not at all. Please, Father, can't I just go back to my nice warm bed. I need my medicines. And all the bacteria in this room is no good for… *(The KING shoves the gag back into his mouth.)*

KING. *(Aside to TRUFFALDINO:)* He seems worse.

TRUFFALDINO. I don't understand I—

FATA MORGANA. Don't you, fool?

> *(FATA MORGANA cackles, throwing off the disguise that let her blend in with the crowd and revealing the sorceress underneath. There is a collective gasp.)*

TRUFFALDINO. Who let you in here, you old wi-atch?

FATA MORGANA. Foolish clown. You know you are no match for Fata Morgana. *(Chord.)*

TRUFFALDINO. We'll see about that, FAT-a MORON-a.

> *(FATA MORGANA goes to slap him and TRUFFALDINO ducks and avoids it. Everyone else on stage, however, reacts as if they*

were slapped. MORGANA, remembering that she has magic, begins to power up for a big zap. Everyone on stage cowers and ducks to avoid the gruesome scene except the NARRATOR and TARTAGLIA. As MORGANA gets a running head start, the NARRATOR trips her and she falls forward, bounces off the cowering TRUFFALDINO and flips over revealing her knickers and striped stockings a la The Wizard of Oz. *The rest of the crowd looks up only in time to see her on the ground and TRUFFALDINO looking down at her and begins applauding and hailing him as the hero. The NARRATOR begins to shush everyone and soon the only sound is that of TARTAGLIA who has been laughing hysterically since she fell over. Everyone in the court begins to celebrate anew with the exception of LEANDRO, BRIGHELLA, and CLARICE who sneak off. SMERALDINA helps a fuming MORGANA up.)*

KING. Truffaldino, you have saved my son! You get the prize!

(He hands him the sack of gold. General rejoicing and applause on stage.)

FATA MORGANA. Stop this! Silence!

(Most of the crowd is silenced, though TARTAGLIA still laughs. MORGANA zaps his arms so they are frozen behind him and he begins to listen attentively.)

Listen to me, you braying ass.

There is one thing they know from Berlin to Montana.
It is never wise to cross Fata Morgana. *(Chord.)*
Enjoying yourself? Getting caught in my verse?
Well, it's more than just poetry. This is a curse.
You've never known love? Here's a present from me.
You'll fall in love with an orange. Better yet, make it three!
I know just the oranges! But don't hold your breath.
They're in the castle of Creonta where you'll meet your death.
Nothing else with suffice, not cheese or soda fizz.
Because the cause of your death will be the love of three oranges!

TARTAGLIA. *(Possessed:)* My precious oranges! I'm coming! I'm coming my dears!

(He rushes offstage.)

FATA MORGANA. Run! Run! Find them if you can!

(She laughs triumphantly, then disappears in a poof of smoke.)

KING. Tartaglia! Stop! Stop him, Pantelone! My son!

(General confusion on stage. Everyone runs off in different directions. The NARRATOR is the only one left.)

Scene 4

NARRATOR. Despite his father's pleading, Prince Tartaglia set off on his quest that very night. Refusing the royal guards, he drafted an unwilling Truffaldino as his squire and only companion for the journey. Fueled by the obsession to find the oranges, they travelled for many days until they finally came upon the castle of the witch Creonta.

> (He turns the page to reveal Creonta's castle and exits. TRUFFALDINO and TARTAGLIA enter riding hobby horses. TARTAGLIA is wearing homemade armor cobbled together from pots and pans from the royal kitchen. Throughout this scene, TARTAGLIA treats his hobby horse as a real horse, moving it as a puppet. TRUFFALDINO treats his like a hobby horse, tossing it on the ground, etc.)

TARTAGLIA. There it is! The castle of Creonta.

TRUFFALDINO. Well, then come on. Let's get this over with. We'll just go get those stupid oranges and then we can finally go home.

TARTAGLIA. They say the castle is guarded by four unspeakable horrors.

TRUFFALDINO. Wait a minute, no one said anything about something unspeakable. What kind of horrors are we talking about here?

TARTAGLIA. It doesn't matter. I am determined to save those three wonderful oranges that I love.

> (TRUFFALDINO is terrified and is not moving an inch.)

TARTAGLIA. Good heavens, man! Are we not heroes! Heroes must be brave no matter what the odds. What of all the damsels in need of rescuing?

TRUFFALDINO. Oh, I'm all about rescuing damsels. I'm just not that willing to risk my life for a few pieces of citrus is all. This whole venture is beginning to sound very dangerous to me.

TARTAGLIA. Servant! I order you to come with me!

TRUFFALDINO. Now wait just a minute! I didn't mind coming here to save you from the first curse, but I am the great Truffaldino, not your servant. I don't care what I promised the wizard Celio, I'm out. I'm taking my sack of gold and going home. You're the one who wants the damn oranges, you go.

TARTAGLIA. You won't come with me? I thought…I thought we were sort of becoming friends. You're the only friend I've ever had.

(TARTAGLIA *puts his hand on* TRUFFALDINO's *shoulder.* TRUFFALDINO *looks at him. They have a moment.* MUSICIAN *plays something like the opening of the theme from "Cheers." It gets weird. They move away from each other.*)

TRUFFALDINO. Oh, now you've gone and made me feel all guilty. I guess this has been sort of fun in a what-the-hell-is-going-on kind of way. Alright, fine let's go get your oranges.

(TARTAGLIA *ties his horse to the nearest tree,* TRUFFALDINO *discards his and they begin to advance on the rusted castle gate. The* NARRATOR *reappears. He has changed out of his costume from the ball and is now wearing a long overcoat.*)

Scene 5

NARRATOR. The castle of Creonta is fraught with dangers. There is an ancient iron gate rusted by time…

(*Just after* TRUFFALDINO *and* TARTAGLIA *pass through the* GATE, *it springs to life and snaps at them.*)

NARRATOR. A demon donkey…

(*While they are focused on escaping the* GATE, *the* DONKEY *comes at them, braying shrilly.*)

NARRATOR. A crazed cook…

(*With a horrible scream, the* COOK *enters wielding a cleaver. They are surrounded. Back to back, they both draw their swords as the horrors advance. They fight to keep them back.*)

NARRATOR. And a dried old rope woven from evil itself.

(*While they are fighting the others, the* ROPE *slides in unnoticed and begins to surround them.*)

NARRATOR. No one has ever left Creonta's castle alive.

TRUFFALDINO. Oh, sure. Now you tell us!

(*The* ROPE *pulls itself tight. The two are bound together, helpless.* CREONTA's *laughter comes from everywhere and nowhere at once. She appears as an old hag.*)

CREONTA. The prince and his clown, all wrapped up and delivered right to my door! While I'd love to keep them for my collection, I promised Fata Morgana (*Chord.*) that I'd finish these two off for good. Come, my pets, let's tear them apart slowly.

TARTAGLIA. You'll never get away with this. Release us at once and free the three oranges!

TRUFFALDINO. Oh, yeah, because that's going to work.

(CREONTA *and the* HORRORS *laugh and begin to advance.*)

NARRATOR. Our heroes struggled against their bonds but it was no use.

CREONTA. Let's start with a spell for pain! (*She readies a magic blast.*)

NARRATOR. The situation looked bleak indeed.

TRUFFALDINO. (*To the* NARRATOR:) Are you going to just stand there or are you going to help?

NARRATOR. Creonta unleashed a powerful blast of magic.

(CREONTA *fires her pain spell.*)

NARRATOR. But the shot went wide.

(*The blast hits the* HORRORS *and they fall back, writhing in pain.*)

CREONTA. What? It can't be! I never miss.

(*The* HORRORS *are gone.* TRUFFALDINO *and* TARTAGLIA *are free. They run for the unguarded castle door.*)

TARTAGLIA. I'm coming, my dearest oranges!

CREONTA. This can't be happening!

NARRATOR. You see, there was one flaw with the witches' plan for revenge. Our heroes were under the protection of the good wizard, Celio, who was far more powerful than either Creonta or Morgana realized. He was, in fact, guiding the entire tale along in ways she could never have imagined.

CREONTA. (*To the* NARRATOR:) Celio? Ha! Yeah, right. I bet he doesn't even exist! (*To the sky:*) Hey, Celio! If you're such an all powerful wizard go ahead and strike me dead right here, right now. (*To* NARRATOR:) He wouldn't dare.

NARRATOR. Wouldn't I?

(*The* NARRATOR *throws off his coat and reveals himself as the wizard* CELIO.)

CREONTA. You're Celio? But what…how…

(CELIO *unleashes a thunderbolt.* CREONTA *is struck dead.*)

CELIO. (*To the audience:*) Oh, please! Like you didn't know it was me all along.

(TARTAGLIA *and* TRUFFALDINO *reappear pulling a wagon with* THE THREE ORANGES *on it. For the sake of simplicity, the* ORANGES *can also tiptoe along single file, tied together at the waist.*)

CELIO. *(To them:)* Go well, young heroes! The oranges are yours. But should you choose to discover what lies inside your prize, you must be certain there's water nearby or face tragedy. *(Dramatic music.)*

TRUFFALDINO. Yeah, sure, whatever.

(*They exit. Then* CELIO *turns the page to the forest as he narrates to the audience.*)

Scene 6

CELIO. The prince and his squire made the long journey back home with the oranges, but no sooner had they left the shadow of Creonta's castle then the curse began to wear off. As his mind cleared, Prince Tartaglia began to face the question the rest of us have wondered about all along. Now that they had them, what were they going to do with three giant oranges?

(TRUFFALDINO *enters with the* ORANGES, *disheveled and exhausted from travel.*)

TRUFFALDINO. Finally! Hey, your highness, we're almost there! *(Realizes he's alone.)* The prince is really lagging behind. I better wait for him to catch up.

(TWO BUMPKINS *enter unnoticed. The* MUTE BUMPKIN *holds a sign that says "Lake of Much Water" in large letters with an arrow pointing offstage.*)

BUMPKIN 1. This looks like as good a place as any for this sign. Did you bring the hammer?

(MUTE BUMPKIN *shakes his head.*)

I thought you had it.

(MUTE BUMPKIN *shrugs.*)

Just stay here. I'll be right back with it.

(MUTE BUMPKIN *stays, holding the sign, waiting and watching the proceedings.* TRUFFALDINO's *stomach growls loudly.*)

TRUFFALDINO. Man, I'm hungry. *(Notices the* ORANGES.*)* Hmm. No. No, I mustn't. But the curse is over, he probably doesn't even want them anymore. He does have three of them. Maybe if I just eat one.

(He cuts open one of the ORANGES. *Out of it comes* NICOLETTA.)

TRUFFALDINO. Whoa! Who put that in there?

NICOLETTA. The sun! It has been so long since I have seen its gentle rays. Oh, they are so bright and hot! They are too hot! Oh, I am so thirsty! Please give me some water! Quickly. Oh, help me... help me... *(She collapses.)*

TRUFFALDINO. Where can I find some water? Where could there possibly be water around here?

(He doesn't notice the MUTE BUMPKIN *with the sign. The* MUTE BUMPKIN *timidly attempts to get his attention.)*

NICOLETTA. Please, or I will die of thirst. Oh, I am so thirsty. Help me!

TRUFFALDINO. Hold on lady. I'll open another orange and get you some of the orange juice to drink. That'll fix you right up.

(He cuts open another orange, out of which comes LINETTA. TRUFFALDINO *screams and faints.)*

LINETTA. I'm finally free! All those years waiting and finally we've been rescued. I would like a drink, though. Oh the harsh sun! Please, please, give me something to drink. You there, help me...help me...

TRUFFALDINO. *(Jumping back up:)* If only I had some indication of where I could find water!

*(MUTE BUMPKIN *is frantic, trying to shove the sign in his face but* TRUFFALDINO *always turns a moment before he gets there.)*

NICOLETTA. Oh, what a fate. I am dying! I am dying of thirst... *(She goes still.)*

LINETTA. I'm dying, you cruel man. Please! Help me...help me... *(She goes still.)*

TRUFFALDINO. Ladies? *(Tries to revive them unsuccessfully.)* Oh no no no. Maybe if I open the third orange I can use the juice from that to save these two!

(As he is about to cut open the third orange, TARTAGLIA *runs in.)*

TARTAGLIA. Truffaldino! Stop! What are you doing? The wizard said we've got to be near water before we open them. Stop!

*(TRUFFALDINO *runs off sobbing.* TARTAGLIA *begins a dramatic mourning for the girls. Music becomes highly tragic.* MUTE BUMPKIN *hangs his head in sadness and maybe crosses himself or blows his nose.)*

TARTAGLIA. Truffaldino, you fool. What's this? Oh no! These poor young girls. Dead? They were but in the spring of their life and now that life has been plucked off them as feathers off a roasted chicken. Alas! How short is our time upon this earth! *(Calls abruptly offstage.)* Hey! Hey, you! Can we get some clean-up out here?

(Some COUNTRY BUMPKINS *enter.)*

TARTAGLIA. Yeah just get rid of these two won't you, they're bringing the whole scene down.

(The BUMPKINS *drag the two girls unceremoniously offstage. The* MUTE BUMPKIN *watches them go with interest.)*

TARTAGLIA. Truffaldino has abandoned me! I've lost the only friend I ever had and now I only have one orange left. I don't even remember why it was so important that I find these oranges in the first place. Though, it is a particularly nice orange. How big and beautiful it is! How lovely and tender is its skin. I must cut it open and just take a tiny peek at what it holds.

(MUTE BUMPKIN notices and runs to stop him but doesn't make it in time. TARTAGLIA *takes out his sword and opens the last one. Out pops* NINETTA.)

NINETTA. Who took me out of my orange? Oh! I am so parched! Water! Water, please! Please, help me!

TARTAGLIA. Oh yeah! Water! I apparently have no short term memory.

(He begins to panic as TRUFFALDINO *did but stops when the* MUTE BUMPKIN *wallops him over the head with the sign and points to what is written on it.)*

TARTAGLIA. Ah! Thank you, my good man!

(TARTAGLIA runs offstage. The MUTE BUMPKIN *and the dying* NINETTA *look at each other. He gives her a little wave. She gives him a weak wave back. He gets an idea and dashes offstage in the same direction that* TARTAGLIA *just exited. As he exits,* TARTAGLIA *runs back on with one of his shoes filled with water.)*

TARTAGLIA. Excuse the vessel, dear lady, but here's some water.

(She drinks the water, her face buried in the shoe. While she drinks, the MUTE BUMPKIN *comes running back holding a cup of water in each hand. He runs clear across the stage, exiting in the direction the other bumpkins took the first two oranges. When* NINETTA *has drunk her fill, she slowly lowers the shoe and really sees* TARTAGLIA *for the first time. It is instant love. Sappy music to indicate as such.)*

NINETTA. Oh, thank you, most heroic sir. You have saved my life.

TARTAGLIA. Are you OK?

NINETTA. *(Meaning her love:)* I don't think I'll ever be the same. *(Catches herself.)* I mean to say, I've been in an orange.

TARTAGLIA. Please, my dearest lady, let me help you up. So, tell me. What was a girl like you doing in an orange like this?

NINETTA. Well, I wasn't always an orange. I am actually a princess and Ninetta is my name. My two sisters and I were turned into oranges by the wicked witch Creonta. Oh my beloved sisters! How I've missed them in that horrid orange! I do hope they are happy and well. Have you seen them, fair sir?

TARTAGLIA. Uh…no. I just got here myself. I'm sure they are fine. Oh, but Princess Ninetta! You have other things to think about. For I am Prince Tartaglia, my father is the King of Hearts, and I have never known such complete happiness in all my life as you make me feel. Ninetta, I believe I am in love with you. Will you make me this happy forever? Will you marry me and be my Queen of Hearts, since you already rule over mine?

NINETTA. We just met three seconds ago! Isn't this a bit sudden? People certainly do fall in love fast in this story! Though, you are fairly handsome and it's so nice to be a princess again instead of an orange. Oh, heck. OK sure!

> *(He dips her over and they kiss. While mid-kiss,* NINETTA *breaks away, turns to the audience and says:)*

NINETTA. Give me a break. You spend a few years in an orange and see how picky you are! *(Returns to the kiss. To him:)* I feel like we're in a fairy tale.

TARTAGLIA. We are, my jewel, which means we are guaranteed the happily ever after. I cannot wait to present you to my father.

NINETTA. Oh, but this dress is covered in pulp. I have nothing suitable to meet a king in.

TARTAGLIA. My precious, my father will love you no matter how you are dressed, but if you insist, I'll bring the whole court to you along with some fine clothes fit for a princess. Wait here, my love, while I go tell my father about the beautiful creature I promised to marry.

> *(A flurry of kisses throughout this exchange.)*

NINETTA. My love! My dear water boy! I will wait for you.

TARTAGLIA. Yes, yes, my future queen. Wait for me here.

NINETTA. I promise to stay right here.

TARTAGLIA. And I promise to hurry back and marry you.

> *(He exits, a spring in his step at last. The* NARRATOR *freezes* NINETTA *with a clap and then walks onto the stage. He tries to end the play as* MORGANA *sneaks up from behind.)*

CELIO. And so it was that the prince returned to the kingdom with a new bride. They married and Tartaglia finally had someone who could truly touch his heart. As King and Queen, they ruled their kingdom with kindness and laughter and everyone lived happily ever…

FATA MORGANA. Not so fast, Celio! *(She freezes him with a snap.)*

You ruined my revenge but I've planned for all these hours
And now with one simple spell I negate all your powers!
You've been running this show. Every choice was your choice.
Well, I'd like to see you narrate if you don't have a voice!

> *(*MORGANA *snaps to unfreeze him and bursts into evil laughter.* CELIO *tries to continue with his narration but no sound comes out of his mouth. He tries silently shouting at* MORGANA *but she only laughs at him.)*

FATA MORGANA. Oh, try all you wish, Celio, but I figured out your little game. You cannot stop me now! You're powerless. You are one of the characters in the story just like everyone else now. Brighella! Smeraldina!

> *(*BRIGHELLA *and* SMERALDINA *enter.)*

FATA MORGANA. Grab him!

> *(The lackeys grab him and drag him kicking and silently screaming offstage.)*

FATA MORGANA. It's about time we had a fairy tale where evil put up a decent fight. *(To the audience:)* Sorry for the inconvenience, everyone, but I'm telling this story now! And I'm going to make sure that it turns out my way! Miserably ever after for the king and prince. *(Narrating:)* As the princess sat alone in the forest, she was approached by a stranger.

> *(*MORGANA *goes gleefully to sit in the audience where* CELIO *had sat. She unfreezes* NINETTA.)*

FATA MORGANA. Smeraldina! That's you. You're on!

> *(*SMERALDINA *reenters with the magic bobby pin.)*

SMERALDINA. Whoa, honey! You are having one hell of a bad hair day!

NINETTA. Am I? O dear! I'm meeting my fiancé's family soon and I'd really like to look my best. There no mirrors in this forest and I've been in a very awkward position in an orange for a long time.

SMERALDINA. Here, let me fix it for you.

FATA MORGANA. But Smeraldina was actually a servant of Fata Morgana. *(Chord.)* Smeraldina brought out an enchanted hairpin expertly crafted by the beautiful and powerful enchantress herself and placed it into the princess's hair causing her to transform into a dove.

> (SMERALDINA *pins up her hair and* NINETTA *turns into a dove and flies off. This can be accomplished by* NINETTA *manipulating the dove puppet herself while the others simply watch the puppet and ignore the actress.)*

SMERALDINA. *(To* MORGANA*:)* Uh, you want me to try to catch her?

FATA MORGANA. No need, Smeraldina. I am running this story now. In fact, I am tired of waiting. What do you say Prince Tartaglia comes back right now?

> (SMERALDINA *sits on the log and assumes a royal air. Sounds of a royal march are heard offstage. The* KING *enters, with* TARTAGLIA, LEANDRO, PRINCESS CLARICE, BRIGHELLA, PANTALONE, *and the court. Narrating:)*

FATA MORGANA. The Prince returned with his father and all the court to meet his bride. *(Gleeful pause.)* And then he walked into a tree.

> *(He does so.)*

FATA MORGANA. Twice.

> *(He does so again. She laughs with great amusement.* TARTAGLIA *recovers himself and begins.)*

TARTAGLIA. Here she is, father. Here is the princess that I love and want to make my queen. *(He looks at her for the first time.)* GAH! Who are you?

SMERALDINA. I am Princess Ninetta, the girl you promised to marry.

TARTAGLIA. You so are not!

> *(The crowd reacts with shock.)*

SMERALDINA. I never should have trusted you! *(To the* KING:*)* He told me he loved me and he promised he would marry me or I never would have…

> *(She degenerates into exaggerated sobs. Everyone turns accusingly to* TARTAGLIA.*)*

KING. My son, a royal promise is a royal promise. You should not make promises in the heat of the moment that you do not intend to keep in the morning light.

TARTAGLIA. Oh, wait! Ew! You people think that I…and her…? No! I would never even touch…

> *(*SMERALDINA *weeps even louder.* NINETTA *flies back onstage unseen, watching the proceedings.)*

KING. You will marry this woman. I order you to do so!

PANTALONE. But your majesty…

KING. No son of mine will go back on his promise. Let us all go back to the palace. This matter is closed. The wedding will be tonight.

> *(*SMERALDINA *laughs and gives* TARTAGLIA *a kiss on the check and a smack on the backside.)*

TARTAGLIA. Princess Ninetta! My love, where are you?

> *(*NINETTA *tries to fly to him but the* GUARDS *grab* TAR-TAGLIA *and drag him off.* NINETTA, *furious, begins to peck* SMERALDINA *on the head which makes her shriek and run offstage.* FATA MORGANA *laughs riotously.)*

Scene 7

(The stage is clear. MORGANA *starts to end the play.)*

FATA MORGANA. *(Enjoying herself immensely:)* And so it was that the Prince was forced to marry the woman he found in the forest. That night she put a magic bobby pin in his hair too and he turned into a pig whose feet they used for jelly. And the King, at seeing his limping leg-less pig of a son, gouged out his eyes with a brooch. So they lived the rest of their days miserably ever…

CELIO. *(Bursting forward with triumphant music:)* Not likely!

FATA MORGANA. What? How did you get here? How did you get your voice back? This makes no sense.

CELIO. It doesn't have to. See, I know a few things about fairy tales, Morgana, that you seemed to have overlooked. Number 1. Things always look bleaker before they get better. Number 2. Good always wins, no matter the odds. You never really had a chance at all.

FATA MORGANA. Fool! Do you know who you are dealing with? I am Fata Morgana!

    (Instead of the usual chord, there's a strange call from offstage.)

FATA MORGANA. What was that?

MUSICIAN. I think it was some kind of ninja chicken.

FATA MORGANA. What do—

    (TRUFFALDINO appears and repeats the ninja chicken sound. After a quick kung fu warm up, he throws his rubber chicken directly at MORGANA's head. She collapses in a heap.)

CELIO. But most of all, Number 3. Willful suspension of disbelief. Nothing ever has to make sense as long as the audience is amused. Truffaldino, would you do the honors?

    (CELIO drags MORGANA offstage as TRUFFALDINO starts the final scene.)

Scene 8

TRUFFALDINO. OK, everyone let's finish this up so we can all go home! So, Prince Tartaglia is getting married and the King has ordered me to help prepare the wedding feast. But the poor prince is still not happy and won't even talk to his bride. Eh, he's probably better off. That is how most marriages end up anyway. But right now my job is to roast the chicken.

    (TRUFFALDINO starts roasting a rubber chicken on a spit. The dove NINETTA appears.)

NINETTA. Good day, Mr. Cook.

TRUFFALDINO. Well, howdee, little pretty birdie.

NINETTA. I would love for you to fall asleep and burn the chicken so that ugly hag, Smeraldina, does not get to eat any of it.

TRUFFALDINO. Glad to be of service, miss.

    (TRUFFALDINO falls asleep on his feet. PANTALONE enters yelling and awakens TRUFFALDINO.)

PANTALONE. Everyone is hungry, Truffaldino! Where is the chicken? Shouldn't it be ready by now?

(TRUFFALDINO *points to the chicken.* PANTALONE *grabs it and screams.*)

PANTALONE. You've ruined it. It's all rubbery!

TRUFFALDINO. Ok, so I can explain. This huge white dove came in here and asked me to go to sleep.

PANTALONE. And you did so?

TRUFFALDINO. Well she asked so nice!

(NINETTA *reappears.* TRUFFALDINO *and* PANTALONE *chase her. When they finally catch the dove, they discover the bobby pin in her head.*)

PANTALONE. What is this doing here?

TRUFFALDINO. I don't know. I'll pull it out.

(TRUFFALDINO *pulls the pin out and the white dove is transformed into* PRINCESS NINETTA.)

TRUFFALDINO. Dude!

PANTALONE. Gracious!

NINETTA. Oh, thank you so much!

(*The* KING *enters.*)

KING. The wedding guests are all waiting for the main course. Truffaldino, where is the chicken?

(TARTAGLIA *follows, recognizes* NINETTA *instantly, and rushes to her.*)

TARTAGLIA. Princess Ninetta! My Ninetta!

(*They embrace.*)

KING. What is going on here? What is the meaning of this? Who is this girl?

NINETTA. I, your highness, am Princess Ninetta. I was an orange earlier today and then Smeraldina turned me into a dove, until this kind fellow saved me. I am the girl your son promised to marry and I do want to marry him, sire.

TARTAGLIA. Oh, yes! Yes! Yes!

(*He kisses her. The* KING *stands in amazement as* SMERALDINA *enters the kitchen.*)

SMERALDINA. Where is my wedding banquet? I'm hungry. And where is my pookie-wookie prince? He left the table so suddenly.

(LEANDRO, CLARICE, BRIGHELLA, *and the rest of the court follow her in.*)

KING. There has been dirty work afoot. Now why, Smeraldina, did you put a spell on this sweet girl?

SMERALDINA. Me? A spell? Ok, so let me explain. Spell, spell is such a strong word. As is put. Now see, I think I can best explain my thoughts on the matter in a dramatic monologue from Jack Nicholson's character in *A Few Good Men*...

(CELIO *suddenly appears.*)

CELIO. Quiet, Smeraldina. You are the agent of the evil Fata Morgana, who is now dressing her wounds in hell. Leandro, Princess Clarice, and Brighella are also her agents.

KING. Well, random wizard I've never met before, though you present no proof to back up your claims, that entrance was pretty impressive, so I'm going to just take what you say on faith. I order Smeraldina, Leandro, Princess Clarice, and Brighella to all be banished from my court immediately and sent into exile.

(*The palace GUARDS surround all four of them and march them out. They speak the following over each other as they are led out.*)

LEANDRO. You cannot get rid of me that easy! I will be King I will! *(Etc.)*

CLARICE. Owie! Get your hands off me! You're wrinkling my dress! Hey you're cute... *(Etc.)*

SMERALDINA. This sucks! I was so freaking close to being queen... *(Etc.)*

BRIGHELLA. This was fun! I hope we'll be back for the sequel!... *(Etc.)*

KING. And now, let us have a real wedding at last. My loyal subjects! May we take something away from all this silliness, some message from all the chaos. There is no greater power than that of a laugh and happiness is a force which can save a person from the horrors of the world. Tartaglia and Ninetta make each other happy and that in turn should bring us all joy. Let us celebrate the triumph of merriment!

TARTAGLIA. Thank you, father.

NINETTA. Thank you, my lord.

(TARTAGLIA *and* NINETTA *kiss passionately to general merriment and assorted hurrahs on stage. Everyone begins to dance and celebrate.*)

TARTAGLIA. Mmmmm. Citrus!

CELIO. And so the King Tartaglia and Queen Ninetta married and ruled the kingdom for many years to come. And though they never changed the world or brought their kingdom great success overseas, they ruled with laughter and brought joy to their subjects' lives and their own. So I thank you for giving us your time and I hope you had a few smiles in exchange. For this is really the end this time and I can now say with all assurance that everyone lived happily ever in laughter.

End of Play